THE G.I. SERIES

A young Marine is presented with the Navy Cross. The Navy Cross is second only to the Medal of Honor in the Marines'
hierarchy of awards. He is wearing the forest green winter service uniform with peaked garrison cap. Early versions of the
winter service uniform were worn with a cordovan leather garrison belt with brass buckle. Beginning in 1943 the leather
garrison belt was replaced with a cloth belt made from the same material as the jacket. (NA)

THE G.I. SERIES

THE ILLUSTRATED HISTORY OF THE AMERICAN SOLDIER, HIS UNIFORM AND HIS EQUIPMENT

The Marines in World War II

From Pearl Harbor to Tokyo Bay

Christopher J. Anderson

CHELSEA HOUSE PUBLISHERS
Philadelphia

First Chelsea House hardback edition published 2002.

Library of Congress Cataloging-in-Publication Data
(on file)

DEDICATION
Thanks Mom.

ACKNOWLEDGEMENTS
This book would not have been possible without the
assistance of Raymond Dankhaus, John Langellier,
Kurt Lightel, and the members of the USMCHC

Designed by DAG Publications Ltd
Designed by David Gibbons
Layout by Anthony A. Evans
Edited by Stuart Asquith
Printed in China

THE MARINES IN WORLD WAR II
FROM PEARL HARBOR TO TOKYO BAY

Joseph Rosenthal's picture of a group of United States Marines raising the American flag on top of Iwo Jima's Mount Suribachi is, perhaps, one of the most famous images of World War II. It has come to symbolize the courage, devotion and determination of the American people as they waged the most ferocious war in human history. Prominent in waging that war, of course, was the United States Marine Corps. Founded during the American Revolution, the USMC had soldiered on for more than a 150 years prior to the start of World War II as a branch of the Navy Department. During that time it struggled not only against a variety of foreign enemies, but also against those in the United States who believed that the Marine Corps was an irrelevancy that a cost conscious government could ill afford.

Although it had repeatedly demonstrated its usefulness during a variety of wars and in international trouble spots during those years, the Marines had largely escaped becoming the objects of public adoration. All of this began to change during World War I where a Marine Brigade assigned to the United States Army's Second Infantry Division served with great distinction in the final campaigns of the war. Despite their performance in France, however, the Corps spent the two decades between the wars in a constant struggle with a parsimonious Congress to ensure their survival and relevance.

Throughout the 1920s and 1930s legendary Marine commandant John A. Lejuene waged an all out public relations struggle to ensure that the American people would not forget the Marine Corps. Meanwhile, while a war weary American public grappled with the domestic crisis of the Great Depression, military theorists began to grow alarmed by the increasingly aggressive actions of Japan. Always attuned to future threats and casting about for a mission that would ensure their survival, many Marines began to look toward means of combating what they saw as the increasingly bellicose actions of Imperial Japan. Taking advantage of experience gained during its campaigns in Haiti and Nicaragua, Marine strategists began testing theories and doctrines that would become the groundwork for the landing operations used with such effectiveness during World War II. Because of the relatively small size of the Corps, in September 1939 the Marine Corps were

only 20,000 men strong, these training operations were conducted using limited numbers of men and material.

When the Japanese began their lightning advance through Southeast Asia in December 1941, Marine detachments were serving in small detachments in a wide variety of far-flung postings from Iceland to the Philippines. Many of their postings were on some of the United States Pacific holdings, which meant that Marines were among some of the first U.S. forces to come to grips with Japanese forces. By the end of December 1941, despite determined resistance, Marine detachments on Guam, Wake Island and Corregidor had been forced to surrender to superior enemy forces. Although they often faced inevitable defeat during these early encounters with the enemy, the Marines were already demonstrating their resolve and determination in combat and perhaps more importantly, were buying time for a woefully unprepared United States to make the necessary preparations for fighting a global war.

During these first clashes with the enemy, the Marines were equipped little differently than their fathers had been twenty years previously during the Great War. The Marine rifleman stationed on Wake Island, Guam or Corregidor would have been wearing summer service dress uniforms that consisted of khaki cotton shirt, trousers and garrison cap or M1917A1 dishpan helmet with, or without, a Marine Corps Eagle Globe and Anchor (EGA) insignia affixed to the front. Marines serving in colder climes, such as Iceland, would have been wearing the forest green wool service uniform, which consisted of forest green wool trousers, wool flannel shirt, khaki cotton scarf, forest green four pocket coat and peaked service cap. For dress occasions Marines would wear the distinctive dress blue uniform first introduced in 1912, which consisted of a blue jacket piped in red and light blue trousers with either a white, or dark blue cap cover and white or cordovan belt. Despite their popularity, issue of the dress blue uniform was suspended in 1942 because of the rapid rate of the USMC's expansion and to conserve materials. Regardless of the temperature of his posting, however, a Marine would have been equipped with M1912 web equipment (M1928 equipment in army parlance), which was virtually identical to the equipment worn during World War I. Indeed, much of the M1912 equipment in use by the USMC, which only received new equipment after the army and navy, would, undoubtedly, have been remainders from World War I. He would have been armed with the M1903 Springfield Bolt Action Rifle, which had been in service with the USMC for almost forty years.

As isolated groups of soldiers and Marines with inadequate clothing and equipment struggled to stop the Japanese advance, preparations were underway to assemble forces large enough to take the offensive against the enemy. Some much needed new equipment, developed in an effort to improve that upon that used in the last war, began to be issued to Marines who had been serving in the United States at the start of the war. This new equipment included the improved M1 helmet and the new M1941 pack system, which was often referred to by Marines as '782 gear' after the requisition form they were required to sign to recieve it. The new pack system was a great improvement over the M1912 pack. It consisted of a separate top (haversack) and bottom (knapsack) with a set of load bearing suspenders. The new system could be configured in a number of different ways depending upon the tactical situation. In addition, unlike the earlier pack system whose load bearing suspenders used to support the weight of the ammunition belt were integral to the pack, the new Marine pack system allowed for the suspenders to be worn without the packs. The 782 gear proved to be so versatile and popular that it later served as the inspiration for the Army's improved M1943 pack system.

This new equipment was also received by the tens of thousands of volunteers who swarmed recruiting depots and volunteered for service in the Marine Corps. While these 'boots' were being trained in preparation for the offensives to come, disparate units of veterans were being combined into larger formations. During the first months of 1942 the 1st Marine Division, which had been activated at Guantanamo Bay Cuba in February 1942 and nicknamed the 'Old Breed' due to the large numbers of experienced active duty Marines in its ranks, was increased in strength and shipped to the Pacific in March. The 2d Marine Division was activated in February 1942 and had begun to ship to the Pacific as well. Its members were often known as 'Hollywood Marines' because of their original proximity to the movie making capital of the same name. After additional training and preparation the 1st Marine Division made its first landing on a hostile shore when they landed at Guadalcanal in the Solomon Islands chain on August 7, 1942, the 2d Marine Division joined them in November. While much of the equipment used during the initial days of the Guadalcanal operation was identical to that worn on Wake Island eight months previously. Soon improved weapons and equipment began to reach the Marines on Guadalcanal.

Not long after landing the first sets of the famed sage green herringbone twill fatigue uniform began to be received. Originally intended as a fatigue garment that would replace the earlier blue denim fatigue uniform, the utility uniform was approved for issue on November 10, 1941, the Marines' birthday. Although the uniform was not designed to be worn as a combat uniform, its comfort and practicality meant that men in combat were soon using it. The new uniform consisted of a jacket that was closed by four bronze buttons bearing the motto: U.S. MARINE CORPS (in an effort to conserve metal, these buttons were soon made of white metal coated with a black paint). The jacket had three patch pockets, two at the hip and one on the left breast. The left breast pocket was stencilled with the Eagle, Globe and Anchor (EGA) insignia and the letters USMC. The trousers had two slash pockets at the front and two hip pockets in the rear. Early versions of the trousers also had a watch pocket, but this was soon discarded.

Also adopted after the landing on Guadalcanal was the semi-automatic M-1 Garand rifle. Although the Garand had been in service with the army for six years prior to the Guadalcanal operation, it had not begun to be received by the Marines of the 1st and 2d Divisions until well into the campaign for the island. Although many Marines at first frowned upon the Garand, claiming that the earlier 03 was more accurate and reliable, the rifle's superior firepower guaranteed its eventual acceptance. By the end of 1943 it had become the Marines' primary infantry weapon.

Marines on Guadalcanal, with the assistance of the army's 25th Division, which arrived in December, battled the Japanese for another six months before finally securing the island in February 1943. Although the victory had been costly, the First Marine Division had suffered almost 3,000 battle casualties; the victory at Guadalcanal stopped the Japanese advance toward Australia and New Zealand and gave American forces a jumping off point for renewed offensives in 1943 against the remainder of Japanese holdings in the Solomons.

Among the changes in the Marines appearance as a result of lessons learned during the campaign was the introduction of camouflage items to the combat uniform. Although the majority of the Marines on Guadalcanal had been wearing either khaki service uniform or sage green utilities, some, particularly artillery and rear area troops, had received the Army's one-piece camouflage uniform. Like their Army comrades, Marines complained about the one-piece suit's weight, and inconvenience when nature called. In response to these criticisms, the USMC began developing camouflage clothing of its own. By the end of 1942 the camouflage helmet cover, which became a trademark of the combat Marine, began to be introduced. The cover was made of the same 'frog pattern' camouflage used on the one-piece army uniform. The horticultural editor of *Better Homes and Gardens* had developed the frog pattern camouflage for use on Army uniforms. The camouflage was reversible with one side having predominantly green shades and the other predominantly brown. It should be noted that the first model helmet cover did not have any insignia stencilled onto it, although many Marines stencilled their names and the EGA insignia to the cover.

So equipped, the Marines continued their reconquest of the Solomon Islands. First Rendova fell, then New Georgia and finally, the Japanese hold on Bougainville was broken by the newly arrived 3d Division in November 1943. While Marine and army units slowly began to regain ground in the Solomons, Marines began to receive additional equipment that had been developed based on lessons learned during the war's early battles. By the end of 1943 camouflage shelter halves had replaced the earlier drab ones. In addition, HBT fatigue hats, initially received from the army, began to be issued with the utility uniform. Being very proud of their service and wanting to distinguish themselves from soldiers, many Marines took to pinning a bronze EGA to the front of their caps. The end of the Solomons campaign also saw the introduction of the utility knife, more popularly known as the 'K-Bar' fighting knife.

Although a variety of other clothing was worn by a variety of specialized units by late 1943, the uniform of the World War II Marine was, essentially complete. Among the specialty clothing, however, was the two-piece camouflage utility uniform. This was an almost identical copy of the sage green utilities. Like the helmet cover, the utility uniform was reversible from green to brown. Originally intended for use by the elite raider units, by the end of 1943 the camouflage utility uniform began to be issued to ordinary Marine infantry units. The camouflage uniform was issued sometimes as a complete set and sometimes mixed with the sage green utilities. Many members of the Second Marine Division were wearing the camouflage utility uniform as they stormed ashore onto Betio Island on Tarawa Atoll in the Gilbert Island chain on November 20, 1943.

The struggle for Tarawa Atoll was a gruesome and bloody affair. Despite a tremendous preliminary naval bombardment, Marines suffered horrendous casualties. One reason for the tremendous casualties was that the Landing Craft Vehicle and Personnel (LCVP) that were responsible for landing the majority of the Marines became lodged up on coral reefs off shore and were forced to unload heavily laden Marines far from the beach. Disembarking Marines had to advance almost 700 yards, the entire time under enemy fire, before they even arrived on the beach. The Marine's first wave suffered seventy percent casualties and by the end of the battle more than 3,000 Marine and navy personnel had become casualties. Despite the heavy losses, valuable lessons were learned that were used during later assault landings. As historians Jeter Isely and Philip Crowl later explained, 'The capture of Tarawa, in spite of defects in execution, conclusively demonstrated that American amphibious doctrine was valid, that even the strongest island fortress could be seized'.

New tactics, equipment, and techniques had been tried and tested. What worked was retained, what did not was discarded. In addition to changes in uniforms, equipment and doctrine, the very nature of who a Marine was had changed. While prior to the war the Marines had been the preserve of white men, by 1943 African Americans and women had been accepted into the Corps. Under orders from then Secretary of the Navy Frank Knox, African Americans were accepted into the Marine Corps for the first time beginning in 1942 and trained in segregated units commanded by white officers at Montford Point, North Carolina. Although relegated primarily to stevedore and ammunition companies, the almost 20,000 African Americans who became Marines during the war served with distinction. After their participation in the amphibious assault on Saipan Marine Commandant Alexander Vandegrift said, 'The Negro Marines are no longer on trial. They are Marines, period'. Another change was the enrollment of women. Although the last service to create a women's reserve, by 1943 the demands of supplying trained Marines to the expanding war in the Pacific necessitated the creation of the USMCWR. Enticed by the slogan, 'Be a Marine, Free a Marine to Fight,' by the end of the war more than 18,000 women were serving in a variety of capacities in the United States. Significantly, this is slightly more than the number of Marines required for the formation of a full strength division. Despite the creation of specialised units such as raiders and paratroopers and the vast expansion of the Marine air wing, it was riflemen who remained the backbone of the Marine Corps. Although its first under strength division had only come into existence early in 1941, by the beginning of 1944, the Marines had raised five full strength divisions (a sixth was created in September 1944), as well as a number of independent brigades, defense battalions and a vastly expanded air wing.

1944 began with the 4th Marine Division's assault on Kwajalein in the Marshall Islands, which was followed by landings at Eniwetok. After the liberation of the Marshalls, the Marines turned to the Marianas Islands, the first of which to fall was Saipan. By the end of July the Marines were ready for the assault on Guam, which had been taken by the Japanese from a tiny Marine garrison in 1941 and was the first American territory to be liberated. By August 1944 with the conquest of Tinian, the Marianas had been liberated.

Intended to protect the flank of General Douglas Macarthur's invasion of the Philippines, the Marines next landing was on Peleliu in September 1944. Marines of the 1st Marine Division fought against more than 13,000 enemy soldiers for control of this tiny island seven miles long and only two miles across at its widest point. For more than a month the Marines and later an Army regiment, battled with the Japanese defenders before the island could be secured. Although it was argued that the assault on Peleliu was unnecessary, it did give Marine planners a sense of what to expect when they attacked their next target; Iwo Jima.

Iwo Jima is a small lamb-chop shaped volcanic island in the Bonin Island group, which is slightly more than 600 miles southeast of Japan. Despite its small size, (the island is only four miles long and two and a half miles wide) and inhospitable terrain (the majority of the island is covered in volcanic black sand), its location so close to Japan was critical to Allied planners who intended to use the island's two airfields for fighter planes that could escort B-29 bombers all the way to the home islands. Aware of the island's importance, Japanese planners had honeycombed Mount Suribachi, and much of the rest of the island with formidable defenses. They had garrisoned the island, with 23,000 experienced soldiers determined to perish to the last man rather than surrender. Three Marine Divisions were assigned the task of taking the island. The assault began on February 19, 1945 and the fighting was fierce. Two Marine Divisions, the 4th and 5th, advanced inland and at 10:20 a.m. on February 23d, in what is perhaps one of the most stirring moments in the history of the Marine Corps, the American flag was raised on top of Suribachi. Witnessing the flag raising, Secretary of the Navy James Forrestal said, '*The raising of that flag on Suribachi means a Marine Corps for the next 500 years*'.

The flag raising, however, did not mean an end to the fighting. Marines continued to fight and die, until the Japanese commander, Tadamichi Kuribayashi committed suicide on March 26. The fighting had been brutal. Marine units had suffered more than 24,000 casualties, making it the costliest battle in Marine Corps' history. More men became casualties in the struggle for Guadalcanal than had been in the Marine Corps in 1939.

The struggle for Iwo Jima had been the culmination of all of the years of training and struggle that preceded it. Unlike earlier amphibious assaults, which had often been marked by poor logistics, inadequate naval gunfire and insufficient air support, the amphibious assault on Iwo had been a textbook operation and despite the horrendous losses, victory had been achieved. One participant recollected, '*The landing on Iwo Jima was the epitome of everything we'd learned over the years about amphibious assaults*'.

Having learned valuable lessons from each previous invasion, the Marines had used a number of new items of equipment during the struggle for Iwo Jima, including rocket launchers mounted on trucks and Sherman tanks equipped with flamethrowers to subdue the enemy. In addition, the M1944 utility uniform began to be seen in limited numbers. Developed in response to experiences learned earlier at Tarawa, the new utility uniform featured a large map pocket on the left breast, with a smaller patch pocket over that. The trousers of the new utility uniform featured thigh pockets and a butt pocket. It was intended that the improved carrying capacity of the new uniform would allow Marines to more comfortably carry items normally carried in the haversack into battle. Despite the innovative design of the new uniform, very few sets

reached front line Marines before the final amphibious operation of the war; Okinawa.

Coming just six days after the end of the fighting on Iwo Jima, in the largest amphibious operation of the Pacific campaign, American forces landed on Okinawa after an intensive air and naval bombardment. Having been Japanese territory since before the war and within easy range of allied aircraft, Japanese resistance was fierce. For more than two months, army and Marine units struggled to defeat the Japanese defenders of the island. Fighting continued until 22 June when the final pockets of Japanese resistance were overcome. In the war's final cataclysmic engagement, the Marine, army, and navy units suffered a total of 12,500 dead, the Japanese lost an estimated 110,000 killed. Seventy two days after the final shots were exchanged on Okinawa, representatives of the Imperial Japanese household signed the documents of surrender on board the American battleship USS *Missouri* in Tokyo Bay.

As Secretary Forrestal had remarked at Iwo Jima, World War II had forever ended the question of the value of the United States Marine Corps. Despite their small size in comparison to the Army and Navy, the Marines' contribution to the final Allied victory in the Pacific had been awesome. Beginning with a strength of slightly more than 20,000 men, the Marines had expanded to 485,833 men and women by the end of the war 91,718 of whom had become casualties, eighty of whom had received the Medal of Honor. Despite the radical changes that the organization went through between 1941-1945, the Marine Corps had been able to indoctrinate the hundreds of thousands of young volunteers with the same values and traditions that had maintained it for more than a 100 years. In so doing, they created an elite fighting force that would become an important component in the defeat of Imperial Japan and an integral part of American national security for generations to come.

FOR FURTHER READING

Brown, L.A. *The Marines's Handbook*. Annapolis, The United States Naval Institute, 1940.

Gailey, Harry A. *Historical Dictionary of the United States Marine Corps*. Lanham, MD, The Scarecrow Press, 1998.

Moran, Jim. *U.S. Marine Corps Uniforms and Equipment in World War 2*. London, Windrow and Green, 1992.

Moskin, J. Robert. *The U.S. Marine Corps Story*. New York, Little Brown and Company, 1992.

Rottman, Gordon and Chappell, Mike. *US Marine Corps, 1941-1945*. London, Reed Consumer Books, 1995.

Smith-Christmas, Kenneth L. 'The Marine Corps Utility Uniforms of World War II'. *Military Collector and Historian*, Winter, 1991, Vol. XLIII, No. 4.

Various Authors. *Marines in World War II Commemorative Series*. Washington, D.C., History and Museums Division, Headquarters, U.S. Marine Corps.

Left: A Marine corporal wearing Dress 'B' Blues stands sentry at a stateside installation during WWII. Although its use was suspended in 1942 except for use on specific details, such as recruiters, the dress blue uniform remained a powerful and recognizable symbol of the United States Marine Corps throughout World War II. The Marine is armed with an M1903 Springfield rifle and bayonet. (USN)

Right: Marine rifleman R. W. Cunningham holds his M-1 Garand rifle and kneels before his complete kit prior to his departure for the Pacific Theater. Of special interest is the camouflage shelter half (visible over his right shoulder), which was made of a reversible 'frog' camouflage pattern with green predominant on one side, and brown on the other. Helmet covers and ponchos featured the same pattern of camouflage. (USN)

Three pilots of Marine Torpedo Bombing Squadron 232 relax in front of a sign that highlights their squadron's achievements. The pilots wear a variety of clothing. The pilots on the right and left are wearing herringbone one-piece coveralls, while the pilot in the center is wearing an Army lightweight summer flying suit. All three men are wearing the famous Marine 'Boondocker' service shoe. The rough side out boondocker was the standard combat footwear of all Marines in the Pacific Theater. (USN)

Right: First Lieutenant H. Feehan salutes the colors during an inspection at the Navy Nurse Indoctrination School in October 1943. The Marines are all wearing the winter service uniform. Originally intended for use as both a field and dress uniform during World War II, the service greens served primarily as a dress uniform. Dark cordovan colored shoes are worn by Feehan and the other Marines. Repeated polishing would often give leather shoes and belts a black appearance. (USN)

Right: A Marine 75mm Pack Howitzer shells enemy positions on Torakina Field, Bougainville in December 1943. Several of the crewmen are wearing herringbone twill camouflage utility trousers, part of the camouflage utility uniform first introduced in 1943. Although initially intended to be worn by the Marine's elite raider units, the camouflage utilities soon fell into more general use. This crew proudly displays a captured Japanese battle flag, visible behind the man standing second from the right. (USN)

Right: Continuing a tradition dating back to the eighteenth century, Marines provided security detachments for U.S. naval vessels. In addition, the Marine detachment was also responsible for manning some of their ship's guns. Here, two Marines assigned to one of the USS *Alaska*'s 5-inch guns keep a lookout for the enemy. The Marine at left is wearing an unofficial baseball cap, while the Marine at right is wearing a Navy utility cap to which he has attached his USMC insignia. (USN)

Above: A wounded Marine is treated with blood plasma on Betio Island during the brutal 1943 Tarawa battle. He is being cared for by a Navy corpsman (left) and, most likely, a Marine (right). Since the Marine Corps falls under the administration of the United States Navy Department, Navy medics were assigned to duty with Marine combat units and would wear USMC utility uniforms during operations. The ferocious nature of the Pacific war meant that, in general, Japanese soldiers offered no special treatment to Navy medics. As a result, medics discarded their Red Cross insignia and would paint subdued discs on their helmets, visible on the helmet of the man seated at left, to identify their role. (NA)

Left: 2d Marine Division commander Maj. Gen. Julian C. Smith, rests under the shade of a palm tree on Tarawa in November 1943. General Smith is wearing a khaki cotton summer service shirt and herringbone trousers. Both items are identical to those worn by enlisted personnel. The photograph demonstrates the relaxed attitude taken by Marines, even senior officers such as Smith, during combat operations. (USN)

Right: Brigadier General Harry Schmidt, assistant to the Commandant of the Marine Corps, poses for a formal picture in 1942. Schmidt is wearing the officer's version of the winter service uniform and winter garrison cap. Although made of a finer elastique material than the enlisted versions, the officers' jacket was the same forest green color as worn by enlisted Marines. Officers could wear their winter service jackets with either cordovan leather 'Sam Brown' belt, or a cloth belt, as pictured here. (USN)

Above: Marines and sailors study a relief map of Betio Island en route to the Tarawa operation in 1943. The men are wearing a combination of the herringbone twill utility uniform and khaki cotton service shirts and trousers. Several of the men are also wearing the cotton summer garrison cap. Enlisted men would affix a USMC insignia to the left side of the garrison cap, officers the right. To aid identification, many Marines would stencil their names on their utility uniform. Such a stencil can be seen on the man with his back to the camera at left, as well as on the medic on the right of the picture. (USN)

Below: A Marine Landing Vehicle Tracked (LVT) 4 'Alligator' advances inland during the action on Saipan in June 1944. Although they never seemed to be available in sufficient numbers, LVTs, which could travel in both water and land, afforded Marines some protection as they landed on hostile shores. The LVTs could carry twenty combat ready Marines from ships off shore onto enemy held beaches, allowing their passengers to arrive at the scene of action dry and ready to fight. (USN)

Right: Three navy personnel stand guard over a supply point on a recently secured pacific island. In the left foreground are two USMC 'jerry cans.' These versatile cans were developed as improved versions of the German gasoline can. The cans have been painted in the Marine Corps unique forest green shade, which all vehicles, artillery pieces and miscellaneous equipment were supposed to be painted. (USN)

Below: Never used in the numbers seen in Europe, tanks did prove useful in supporting infantry operations and in reducing Japanese strongpoints. This 1st Marine Division M4 Sherman tank burns after being destroyed by a Japanese mine on Okinawa in June 1945. Marine tankers were equipped with U.S. Army tankers M6 leather crash helmet. Marine tank crews would often attach wooden planks to their tanks to prevent Japanese soldiers from affixing magnetic mines to the sides of the tanks. (USN)

Right: A Marine brings in two Japanese prisoners on Saipan, July 1944. The savage pace of the fighting meant that prisoners were not frequently taken, by either side, during the war. Just visible on the chest of the guard at the rear is the Marine's unique round identification 'dog tag' discs. These discs were different from those of the army, which had a more rectangular shaped disc. (NA)

Below: Marines unload from their Landing Craft Vehicles and Personnel (LCVP) and advance toward the enemy defenses at Tarawa during *Operation Galvanic.* The Tarawa landings proved to be among the most difficult of the war. Marines were forced to wade through chest deep water for a half mile, the entire time under enemy fire, before reaching the beach. After the island was secured, General Julian Smith commented of his Marines that, '*Their only armor was a khaki shirt.*' Many of the men of the 2d Marine Division, which spearheaded the Tarawa landings, were wearing the two-piece camouflage utility uniform. (USMC)

Above: A group of Marines arrive in Shanghai in August 1937. They are all wearing the khaki cotton service uniform with khaki ties, (skarfs in USMC parlance). They are also wearing M1917A1 helmets, to which they have affixed the USMC eagle, globe, and anchor insignia. These helmets would have been painted in the Marines' particular forest green shade. Over the meat can pouch of their M1912 packs they have hung their P1912 Campaign Hats. The famous campaign hat would be discontinued soon after the outbreak of the war. (USN)

Below: A member of the Sixth Marines on duty in Iceland during 1942 works inside one of the Nissan shelters. He is wearing the forest green wool service trousers, unlike army trousers, Marine trousers did not have hip pockets. Despite being inside, he is wearing a wool winter cap, first issued for service in China. Just visible underneath the collapsible table is a well-polished pair of service shoes. (USMC)

Above: Marines in Iceland line up for chow. A variety of both old and new clothing is being worn. The Marine at the head of the line is wearing the blue denim bib overall, which was issued prior to the introduction of the olive drab utility uniform made famous later in the war. The two men serving the food are both wearing the peaked wool service cap, while the fifth man in line is wearing the campaign hat. (USMC)

Below: A group of Marines on an exercise in the frozen conditions of Iceland. With the exception of the Marine standing second from the right in service cap and wool overcoat, these men are all wearing the special P1907 wool cap dating to the First World War and denim fatigues. (USMC)

Right: A USMC film crew sets up their camera in Iceland. The sudden nature of their deployment, and the lack of sufficient winter stores, meant that the Marine Corps was forced to improvise much of the clothing worn by its members in Iceland. Prior to deployment, the Marines purchased a large quantity of winter coats from Sears & Roebuck, seen here being worn by the two cameramen standing at left and center. The Marine at right wears the standard issued forest green wool overcoat. (USMC)

Below: A group of Marines enjoy some time off duty in downtown Reykjavik. Visible on the shoulders of two of the men is the famous Polar Bear Patch. Members of the Marine Brigade in Iceland wore this patch, originally the insignia of the British 79th Division. Unlike shoulder patches worn later in the war, which were worn only on the left shoulder, the Polar Bear patch was worn on both the left and right shoulders. (USMC)

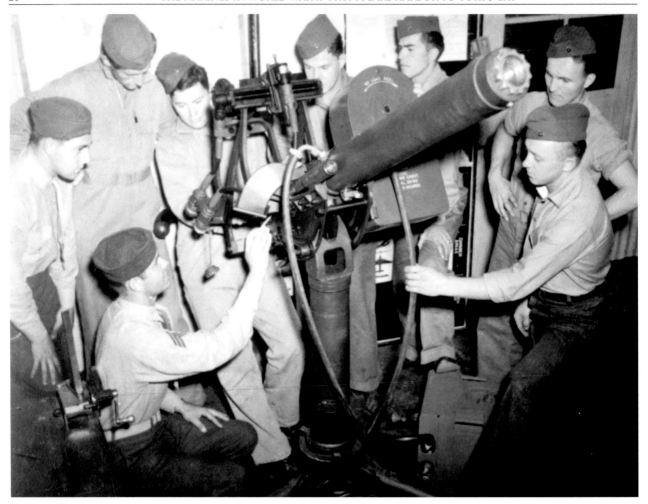

Left: A group of Marines receive instruction on the operation of the .50 caliber anti-aircraft machine gun in the spring of 1942. The Marines are all wearing a variety of fatigue and service clothing. The Marine at right is wearing the khaki cotton shirt with a pair of the early blue denim fatigue trousers, while the sergeant kneeling at left is wearing forest green wool service trousers. The Marine harnessed to the gun is wearing the one-piece herringbone twill fatigue suit. (NA)

Right: Two Marine segeants from the ship's detachment of the USS *Wasp* prepare for inspection in June 1942. Marines assigned to ships' detachments were known for their precision in drill and perfection in appearance. Both of these men are wearing shooting medals on their dress blue uniforms. Just visible on the right sleeve of both men are, from top to bottom, gun pointer first class and expert gunner qualification badges. (NA)

Left: A group of Marines enjoy a brief respite during the defense of the Island of Corregidor in 1942. These men are all wearing the khaki cotton shirt and trousers. The insignia visible on the left shoulder of two of the men at right would have been constructed of the same forest green wool used for the service uniform sewn to a cotton backing. Later in the war, the stripes would have been embroidered directly to a khaki backing. The M1917A1 helmets of two of the men have the EGA insignia attached to the front of the helmet. (USMC)

Left: A young Marine poses for a picture in his herringbone twill utility uniform. Introduced late in 1941 and originally intended strictly for fatigue use, the 'utilities,' would become the most common USMC uniform of the war. The jacket was a loose fitting garment that featured three patch pockets, the one on the left breast bearing the USMC's initials and M1936 insignia stencilled in black. It was closed by four bronze buttons bearing the legend U.S. MARINE CORPS around its outside edge. Soon after the jacket's introduction, however, the buttons began to be manufactured of blackened steel to conserve bronze. (CJA)

Right: A stretcher party evacuates a wounded comrade from the jungles of Guadalcanal. The two men at the front of the stretcher are wearing the herringbone utility uniform, while the man at the left rear is wearing a sweat stained khaki cotton shirt. The campaign for Guadalcanal marked the first time that the herringbone utility uniform was worn as a combat garment and it was worn interchangeably with the earlier khaki cotton shirt and trousers. (USMC)

Right: Marine signalmen in jeeps try and lay communications wire through a muddy Guadalcanal track. Two of the jeep drivers are wearing army HBT Daisy Mae fatigue hats to ward off the sun and heat. Prior to the introduction of the mechanics' hat, this could be seen being worn by some Marines in the field, often with insignia attached. (USMC)

Right: A Marine ground crew put out a fire on one of the Cactus Air Force's Grumman F4F Hellcats during the struggle for Guadalcanal. The Cactus Air Force was comprised of a handful of aircraft that supported Marine operations from Henderson Field. These Marines are wearing a combination of khaki cotton service uniform and herringbone utilities. Of special interest is the M1917A1 helmet being worn by the man working with the shovel second from the right. (USMC)

Above: Three M3A1 light tanks move up on Guadalcanal. Although it was found to be too lightly armored and armed for extensive service in Europe, the M3A1 did see a good deal of service with Marine tank units in the Pacific. The M3A1 featured a 37mm gun and three .30 caliber Browning machine guns. To guard against enemy sniper activity, these vehicle crewmen are all wearing M1 helmets. (USMC)

Below: Three Marine LVT1 'Alligator' landing vehicles bring supplies to the Guadalcanal Beach. The LVT1 was the first model of the famous amphibian tractor (AMTRAC) landing vehicles used with such effectiveness throughout the campaign in the Pacific. It was first used during the Guadalcanal campaign. The alligator's three-man crew could bring 4,500 tons of equipment, or twenty combat ready Marines, on to a beach with dry feet. (USMC)

Above: Much of what gave Guadalcanal such strategic importance was the airstrip at Henderson Field. This building, known as the 'Pagoda', seen here in 1942, served as headquarters for Marine and Navy aviators throughout the heaviest fighting for the island, but eventually had to be torn down after suffering damage during a Japanese air raid. (USN)

Right: During a lull in the fighting, a Marine keeps watch for Japanese soldiers while men of the 1st Marine Division take a bath in the Lunga River. The machine gunner is wearing the HBT utility uniform. By his left side is an olive drab two man tent, constructed of two halves, which is used here as shelter for the machine gun position. The camouflage shelter half, often seen rolled onto the Marines' pack did not come into use until 1943. (USN)

Left: This Paramarine is kitted out for a jump. Underneath his M1 helmet is the leather jump helmet. Unlike the Army's special M1C jump helmet, the USMC wore a standard M1 helmet over the leather jump helmet. Another variation between Army and Marine parachutists was the jump boots. Unlike those worn by the Army, Marine jump boots did not have a toecap. (NA)

Right: Lieutenant Colonel Evans F. Carlson back on board the submarine USS *Nautilus* after returning from the Makin Island Raid, the first Marine Raider action of the war. A career military man who saw service in both the Army and Marine Corps, Carlson founded the elite Marine Raider battalions after his service with the Chinese Communists prior to America's entry into the war. Carlson is wearing standard three pocket Marine utility uniform He is supporting his pistol belt with a pair of M1936 Army suspenders. (NA)

Below: A couple of Marine Raiders pose in front of a Japanese torpedo on Guadalcanal in February 1943. The Marine at left is wearing one of the khaki cotton shirts died black with khaki trousers while the sergeant at right is wearing the three pocket sage green utility uniform and cotton garrison cap. (NA)

Above: Raiders stand on deck as the USS *Argonaut* enters Pearl Harbor after the Makin Raid. While some of these men are wearing navy denim fatigue clothing, most are wearing khaki cotton shirts and trousers died black. Prior to the Makin Raid, each member of the Second Raider Battalion received one set of black khakis for use during the raid. (USN)

Below: Raider commander Carlson in June 1943. Carlson is wearing the early papier maché liner and three pocket sage green utility uniform and has pinned his lieutenant colonel's insignia to his collar. It was common during combat operations for officers to forego wearing any insignia. Visible on his utility jacket is the herringbone weave of the cotton material used to make the jacket. Also visible are the U.S. MARINE CORPS buttons used on the utility uniform. (USMC)

Above right: Raiders use a rubber boat during a training exercise in April 1943. All but one of these men is wearing an M1 helmet that has been covered with burlap and loosely woven mesh netting. The raider second from the right has dabbed black paint on his haversack to camouflage it. These raiders are also wearing Navy gasmasks over their shoulders. (USMC)

Right: A communications post somewhere in the jungle. This photograph was taken in April 1943, prior to the issue of camouflage utility uniforms and helmet covers to the raiders. Despite their elite status, there is nothing visible in this photograph that distinguishes these raiders from the typical Marine of early 1943. (USMC)

Left: While most Marines were involved in operations in the Pacific, by 1943 there were detachments of Marines who were serving in the European theater as well. Here, Admiral Harold R. Stark, commander U.S. Navy Forces Europe, inspects a Marine detachment. These Marines are turned out in 'Dress A' blues. Dress A called for dress blue jackets, dress blue frame cap cover, and white gloves and belt. Due to wartime conditions, these Marines are also wearing U.S. Navy Mark III gasmasks slung over their shoulders. Throughout World War II, the Marines maintained a barracks in London. (USN)

Left: Marine guards escort a captured German submariner to a holding cell at Norfolk Navy Yard in June 1943. Since Marines traditionally provided security details on board ship and at Naval installations, they were responsible for escorting German U-boat prisoners brought to Norfolk. These Marine guards are wearing well-pressed summer service khaki cotton shirts and trousers with tropical fiber helmets. These helmets were infrequently seen in the Pacific theater, but continued to be issued, and worn, at stateside recruit depots and Naval installations throughout the war. (NA)

Above: A group of Marines inspect a Japanese anti-aircraft gun after the capture of Lae in September 1943. These men have the newly introduced camouflage helmet covers secured over their M1 helmets. The camouflage helmet cover soon came identify the Marines of World War II. The man seated at right has his trouser legs bloused over his leggings, a common practice among Marines in the field. (USAMHI)

Below: A man armed with an M1 Carbine keeps a sharp eye out for enemy snipers. He is wearing rubber soled jungle boots. Although not frequently worn by ordinary Marines, these did see limited service among raiders and those individuals fortunate enough to obtain a pair. (NA)

Above: Members of 2d Marine Division enjoy a boxing match prior to the Tarawa Landings. Although originally intended to be worn solely by raider units, by 1943 many ordinary Marine units were wearing the camouflage utility uniform. Many of the members of Marine Division that landed at Tarawa were wearing the camouflage suit. Also visible on several of the men in this picture are the low quarter, rough out, 'boondocker' field service shoes. (USN)

Left: 2d Division are pinned down by Japanese fire on the beach at Tarawa in November 1943. As can be seen here, the camouflage uniform was worn side by side with the earlier sage green utility uniform. Just visible on the right hip of the man at left is the Marines' famous 'K-Bar' utility knife, which began to be issued in 1943. (USMC)

Right: A wrecked LVT1 rests along the sea wall at Tarawa's Red Beach Two. Although the LVT's used at Tarawa were able to bring many Marines directly onto the beach, there were insufficient numbers of the vehicles to land everyone. Many unfortunate Marines were forced to wade for more than a half mile in chest deep water, all the time under Japanese fire. (NA)

Below: After landing at Tarawa three Marines advance past a pile of discarded equipment and a Japanese barbed wire obstacle. The Marine at the front is wearing camouflage utility jacket with sage green trousers, while the Marines behind him are dressed in the sage green utility uniform. Some of the newly introduced camouflage shelter halves and rain capes can be seen in the jumble of equipment lying in the sand. (USMC)

Left: A group of Navy corpsmen operate on a wounded Marine on Tarawa. All of these men are wearing sage green utility uniform. White circles, signifying medical personnel, can be seen painted on the helmets of several of the medics and on the right hip of the corpsman kneeling to the left. Just visible on the medic second from the right is the special Paramarine medical bag that was frequently worn by Navy corpsman during assault landings. (USMC)

Below: Marines unload ammunition on the beach at Tarawa. Interestingly, there are several M1912 packs lying in the foreground of the picture. The USMC had ceased to use the M1912 pack system by this time, which would seem to indicate that these packs belong to naval personnel who have come ashore with the Marines. (USMC)

Above: A Marine throws a grenade at an enemy position at Tarawa while a comrade takes a drink from a canteen. The heat, lack of water and intensity of the fighting on many Pacific Islands meant that Marines frequently carried two canteens. (USMC)

Right: A 75mm pack howitzer crew from the 1st Battalion, 10th Marines, provides artillery support during the Tarawa operation. The relatively lightweight pack howitzer, which could fire six rounds per minute, proved ideal for operations on Pacific islands.(USMC)

Left: Marines inspect a destroyed Japanese tank. Just visible on the bamboo post at the left is a Browning Automatic Rifle Belt (BAR) supported by Marine M1941 belt suspenders. The belt could carry twelve, twenty round, magazines for the BAR, which was the standard squad automatic weapon throughout the war. (USN)

Left: Private First Class Rudloff poses with his M4 Sherman tank at the end of the fighting on Tarawa. Although hit several times, Rudloff's Sherman was one of the few tanks to actually survive the entire operation. He is wearing the two-piece camouflage utility uniform. To protect his eyes from the sun, Rudloff is wearing a pair of Army M1943 goggles. (USN)

Above: Marines capture a Japanese pillbox on Betio Island by frontal assault in November 1943. The habit of travelling as lightly as possible can be clearly seen on these Marines. Only the M2 flamethrower operator, visible near the top of the hill, has any equipment on his back. (USMC)

Right: Officers of the 2d Marine Division confer during the Betio assault. The men are all wearing a mixture of camouflage and sage green utility uniforms. The man standing second from the right with his back to the camera is carrying a pair of M3 binoculars in a leather M-17 case attached to his belt. The Marine seated at left has a special 'sniper' helmet cover worn over his helmet. Unlike the standard helmet cover, the sniper cover featured a cloth band for affixing foliage and a mesh veil that could be worn to hide the face. (USMC)

Left: These members of the 2d Marine Division have just waded into the beach at Betio Island from landing craft located 700 yards away. The photograph illustrates all of the additional equipment that a Marine would be required to carry ashore in addition to his personal equipment. While the two men at the left front are carrying ammunition for the .30 caliber browning machine gun in the early wooden ammunition container, others carry additional ammunition for the BAR and wire for field telephones. (USMC)

Opposite page, bottom: Marines guard some of the few Japanese prisoners taken during the Tarawa operation in 1943. Visible on the left sleeves of two of the Marines are military police (M.P.) brassards. These brassards would have been made of navy blue wool with white lettering. Just visible on the left hip of the Marine at extreme left is a M1938 canvas dispatch case used by officers and senior non commissioned officers to carry maps and other papers. (USMC)

Below: Marines coming off the line at Tarawa in November 1943. The man at the front can be identified as a BAR gunner by the belt he is wearing. His weapon is slung over his right shoulder, a captured Japanese Arisaka rifle over his left. Directly behind him is his assistant BAR gunner. The assistant provided cover and assistance in spotting for the gunner in addition to carrying six extra clips of ammunition in a separate pouch; seen here being worn on the chest of the assistant above his belt. The assistant gunner was armed with an M1 Garand rifle. (USMC)

Left: A Marine armed with an M1 carbine on Tarawa prepares to deliver a belt of .30-caliber machine gun ammunition to a neighboring gun. He is wearing his M1 helmet reversed to aid vision. Visible around his neck are a pair of Marine Corps' biscuit identification 'dog' tags. These tags, secured here by a bootlace, were a different shape than army tags. The dog tag provided the Marines name, rank and blood type. Earlier versions also contained home address and a thumbprint. (USMC)

Left: Major General Holland M. Smith, right, discusses the Tarawa operation with Major General Julian C. Smith. Holland Smith is wearing an army issue helmet net over his M1 helmet and a pair of army issue HBT trousers identifiable by the thigh pocket. Julian Smith wears a khaki cotton shirt that has had its left breast pocket modified to accept pens. A Marine issue web waist belt secures his trousers. Unlike Army officers, waist belt buckles, Marine officers' buckles were open faced like the enlisted version. (USMC)

Above: A Marine with his war dog flushes out an enemy soldier. The Marines first used dogs on Bougainville to assist in locating enemy positions and in carrying messages. The handler is wearing camouflage utilities and is armed with an M1 carbine. Hanging from his pistol belt is an M1910 Pick Mattock and carrier. The Pick Mattock was carried by some members of a squad in lieu of the T-handled shovel. (USN)

Above right: The crew of a .30 caliber M1919A4 machine gun crew mans a water filled hole on Bougainville. The men are both wearing their haversacks with camouflage shelter halves attached to the back. The crewman on the left has two first aid packets and a cleaning kit attached to his pistol belt. Just visible on his right hip is a holster for a .45 caliber pistol. (USMC)

Right: Marines and a Navy medic load a Marine wounded on Bougainville onto a landing craft. The two Marines at the front are wearing two-piece camouflage utility uniforms with, as was most common, the 'green side' out. Unlike the sage green uniform, the camouflage utilities were closed with snap fasteners. Visible on the left breast of each jacket is the EGA stencil. (USMC)

Above: Marines descend the ramp of a landing craft infantry (LCI) at Cape Gloucester in late 1943. The LCI was widely used by Marines during its many amphibious operations. (USMC)

Right: A pair of LVT(A)4s moves toward an enemy controlled beach. The LVT4 (A) 4 was based on the LVT4 chassis, but featured a turret from the M8 self-propelled howitzer. The (A)4 had a crew of five men and provided artillery support to Marine landing parties all the way into the shore. (USN)

Opposite page, top: An M3A1 half-track leaves an LST at Cape Gloucester. Unlike their Army counterparts, the crews of Marine half-tracks were known to camouflage their vehicles, as seen here. The M3A1 featured a 75mm gun and several .30 caliber machine guns. This crew has also added a heavy .50 caliber machine gun to provide additional firepower. (USMC)

Above: The crew of the Marine M5 Stuart tank and supporting rifleman seem oblivious to the dead Japanese soldiers in front of their tank. The Marine resting on the barrel of the tank's 37mm gun has attached two canteens to his pistol belt. He is armed with a .30 caliber Thompson sub-machine gun. Extra twenty round magazines are carried in a web carrier visible on his right hip. (USMC)

Below: A Marine machine gun crew fires into Japanese positions on Cape Gloucester. The three men to the right are all wearing the second pattern camouflage helmet cover, which featured foliage slits cut into the fabric. Interestingly, the gunner is wearing an Army issue HBT shirt, distinguishable by the button closure visible at the wrist. (USMC)

Right: After twenty-three days on the line Marines on Cape Gloucester prepare for a rest. The photograph illustrates the dishevelled condition of men in combat. The men's utility uniforms are almost black from dirt and sweat, and most have discarded their helmet covers. USMC)

Below: Marines loaded onto the back of a 2½ ton truck await a trip to a rest area. Several of the men, seated at right, standing at rear and seated second from left, are wearing army issue HBT trousers, which can be distinguished by thigh pockets. (USMC)

Left: Marines prepare to raise the American flag over Cape Gloucester. The Marine standing at left is wearing a single breasted enlisted man's synthetic rain coat, while next to him holding the flag a Marine is wearing the camouflage poncho. Like the helmet cover and camouflage utilities, the poncho was reversible from brown to green. Standing on the wing of the plane at rear, another Marine is wearing the earlier olive drab poncho. (USMC)

Left: Marines honor their fallen comrades on Cape Gloucester in December 1943. Most of the men are carrying their M1 Carbines, which would indicate that there is still a danger posed by lurking Japanese soldiers. Visible on one of the Marines with his back to the camera is a stencil with the man's name. Stenciling of utility uniforms was a frequent practice. (USMC)

Left: Marine LVTs onboard an LST are transported to New Britain in December 1943 to support the invasion. The photograph shows the variety of gear and equipment that LVT crews would store in their vehicles. Crewmen have also attached jungle hammocks from several of the LVTs. (USN)

Above: Marine Corps legend Lewis B. 'Chesty' Puller, right, greets visitors to his headquarters. Puller is wearing HBT utility trousers. The officer to Puller's right has been able to obtain a pair of USMC rough side out paratrooper boots. (NA)

Right: A Marine intelligence officer questions a wounded Japanese soldier while naval corpsmen work to bandage a wound. The intelligence officer is wearing an army HBT utility cap, to which he has affixed a bronze EGA insignia. This officer has also shortened the sleeves of his utility jacket.(NA)

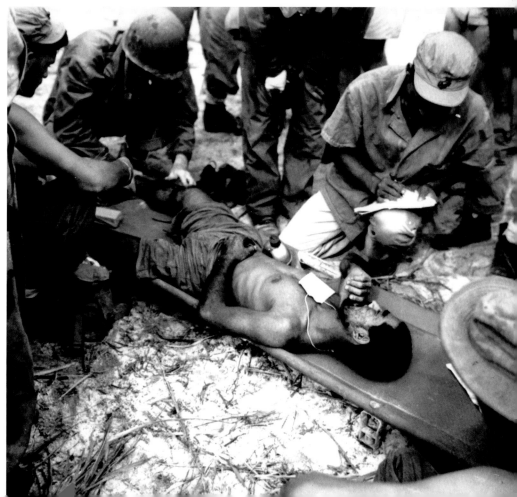

Above: Pilots of the 'Black Sheep' Squadron dash to their planes and prepare to leave from their base at Espiritu Santo in September 1943. The pilots are all carrying their parachutes, with attached M-592 survival kit. The pilot running at left appears to be wearing a pair of Australian Air Force flying boots. (NA)

Opposite page, top: Marine fighter pilot ace Gregory 'Pappy' Boyington briefs his pilots before a mission. All of the pilots are wearing M40 flight helmets with Mk II goggles. Boyington wears a pair of Army issue khaki trousers, identifiable by the pocket visible on right hip. He is also wearing an Army officers' khaki shirt, with shoulder epaulettes that he has modified by shortening the sleeves. (USN)

Left: Members of Boyington's VMF-214 'Black Sheep' Squadron pose in front of one of the units Vought F4U-1 Corsair fighter planes. The photograph illustrates the wide variety of uniforms worn by members of the Marine air wing during active operations. Several of the men are wearing navy issue blue wool baseball caps, while others wear army air corps B-1 caps. (USN)

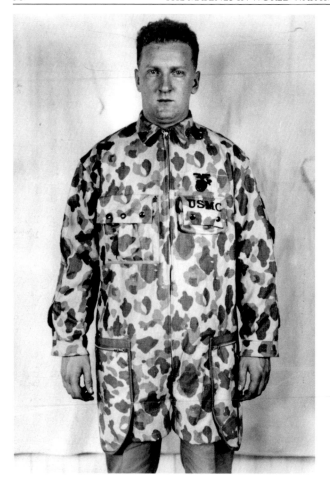

Opposite page, top left: A model wears the second pattern USMC parachute jump smock. The smock was an identical copy of the earlier sage green smock only made from the reversible camouflage material seen on utility uniforms, helmet covers, shelter halves and ponchos. (NA)

Opposite page, top right: An African American Marine, often referred to as a Montford Point Marine, admires his recently awarded Bronze Star. Montford Point was the location of the segregated training base where African American Marines received their training. The Marine Corps was vehemently opposed to the admission of African Americans and they eventually had to be ordered to do so in the summer of 1942. Although relegated primarily to stevedore and ammunition companies, African American Marines did see action on Guam. (NA)

Opposite page, bottom: A group of recently landed African American Marines takes shelter. Visible on the belt of the Marine at the right is the second pattern, crossed flap canteen cover. This model of canteen cover did not begin to reach Marines in the field until 1944. The second pattern featured a large drain hole at the bottom of the carrier. Also visible on the two Marines lying on their stomachs at center are the composite soles of the boondocker boot. The soles were made of a composite material consisting of a mixture of rubber and cotton cord. (NA)

Top right: A Marine on Cape Gloucester in January 1944 sprays the interior of a Japanese pillbox with his .45 caliber M1A1 Thompson sub-machine gun before entering. The Thompson had been used by the Marine Corps since 1922 and despite its weight, remained a popular weapon. It was finally withdrawn from service in 1944. (USMC)

Right: A Marine flamethrower operator stands over the bodies of two Japanese soldiers. He is armed with an M2 flamethrower. He carries a .45 caliber pistol in a M7 shoulder holster as his personal weapon. Flamethrowers were tremendously effective against enemy installations and their operators were frequently targets of Japanese snipers. (USMC)

Opposite page, top: Marines stand guard over a water distribution point on the beach at Eniwetok. The two men crouched by the whole have loose netting over their helmets instead of the more common camouflage cover. The man kneeling at the center is wearing two canteens on his cartridge belt. The canteens are carried in the first pattern canteen cover peculiar to the Marines. This cover resembled the Army model, but was unlined and lacked vertical stitching at the front. (USMC)

Opposite page, bottom: Rear area Marines set up a supply distribution point on Kwajalein. Of particular interest are the boxes at right. All of the wood boxes are stencilled with a half circle. Each Marine division had a special insignia, which was stencilled on equipment, and often on uniforms. In this case, the half circle signifies that these boxes belong to the 4th Marine Division. (USMC)

Above: A Marine .30 caliber machine gun grew follows behind an advancing halftrack during the struggle for Kwajalein in January 1944. While the Marine at front carries the gun, he is followed by two others who carry additional ammunition in wooden cases and, in the case of the man at the rear, in belts draped around his neck and shoulders. The man at the rear has also stenciled the 4th Marine Division Insignia to the back of his utility jacket. (USMC)

Left: Marine pilots of VMF-113, the 'Whistling Devils,' pose beside one of their units' F4U Corsairs after shooting down nine Japanese fighters in March 1944. They are wearing a variety of flying clothing. The man standing second from the right is wearing a lightweight cotton Navy windbreaker with leather nameplate. The pilot third from the left is wearing a three pocket utility jacket that has been modified with the addition of flaps and button closures for each of the pockets. (USN)

Left: A Marine patrol uses demolition charges to flush out a Japanese soldier. The Marine standing third from the right is armed with an M2 flamethrower. The fuel tanks are visible on his back. The flamethrowers importance means that three other Marines are closely guarding him while a fourth goes after the enemy soldier. (USMC)

Below left: Two heavily laden Marines advance across a muddy stream on Guam. The Marine at rear has his 782 gear (Marine parlance for the M1941 pack system) in the field transport pack configuration. This configuration featured the haversack (top), knapsack (bottom), blanket and shelter half. The field transport pack was normally only worn when being transported for long distances and was rarely seen being used during combat operations. More common was the field marching pack configuration, which only involved the haversack, blanket, and shelter half. (USMC)

Below: Marines with a light 37mm cannon support advancing riflemen along the tree line at the right. Although it had been abandoned by Army units operating in Europe due to its light weight, the 37mm gun was ideally suited for use as an anti-personnel weapon in the Pacific. Its three-man crew could fire 15-20 rounds a minute. (NA)

Right: A Marine comes under fire on Saipan 1944. He has strapped rope to the back of his 782 gear. Just visible under the flap of the haversack is his camouflage poncho, which he has folded up. An M1910 entrenching tool is attached to the outside of the pack. The M1910 entrenching tool, commonly referred to as the 'T-handled shovel' remained in use with Marine units longer than with army units, which began to receive the folding shovel in 1943. This Marine has stencilled his name on the outside of his canteen carrier. (NA)

Below: A 105mm howitzer shells Japanese positions on Saipan. The 105mm was a workhorse of both Army and Marine artillery units. A good crew could fire up to four rounds per minute up to ranges of 12,000 yards. By 1944, each Marine division had twelve of these guns. (NA)

Above: A bazooka team shares a foxhole on Saipan. The Marine at the front is armed with an M1A1 Rocket launcher, popularly known as a bazooka. Rockets for the bazooka are carried in the brown cardboard tubes behind the gunner. Also of interest, the assistant bazooka man has the early, 16-inch, bayonet for his Garand rifle. By 1944, most Marines carried the shorter, 12-inch bayonet. (NA)

Below: Marines huddle around an LVT after landing on Saipan and prepare to move out. They are wearing a combination of sage green and camouflage utility uniforms. All of the Marines appear to have come ashore with just their haversacks. According to regulation the haversack would contain a poncho, mess kit, socks, underclothes, sewing kit, towel, shaving kit, extra shoe and legging laces, one 'k' ration, and one 'd' ration. (NA)

Right: A wounded Marine receives blood plasma on the beach at Saipan. An M1 Garand Rifle is used to support the plasma bottle. The Garand was a semi-automatic .30 caliber rifle that was the standard infantry weapon of American armed forces throughout the war. Although received six years later by the USMC than by the army, Marines operating on Guadalcanal in 1942 had been armed with the bolt action Springfield rifle, it would see yeoman service in all of the remaining campaigns of the war. (NA)

Below: Soon after securing the island, the 4th Marine Division established a postal facility for use by its men. Here, a Marine assigned to the post office hands all of a platoons mail to a fellow Marine, who will distribute it to the recipients. (USMC)

Below: A Marine killed during the Tinian operation is laid to rest during a service at sea. The chaplain wears a camouflage utility jacket. At the appropriate moment, the attending Marines will raise the board that the body rests upon, and allow the deceased to slip into the sea. (USMC)

Left: A BAR man advances through the jungles of Tinian. He has attached two canteens to the left side of his BAR pouch. On his back he is wearing the haversack portion of his 782 gear, on to which he has attached his lightweight gasmask carrier. Such heavy loads, the BAR alone weighed almost twenty pounds, made maneuvering thorough thick jungles agony. (NA)

Below: A Marine patrol comes under fire on Tinian. These men are all wearing haversacks with entrenching tools and bayonets attached. They all appear to have the early M1905 bayonet attached to their packs. The M1905 bayonet was sixteen inches long and was carried in a scabbard of wood, canvas and leather. Scabbards such as this were rare by 1944. (NA)

Right: After being relieved, a Marine on Tinian in August 1944 lies on the ground for a rest. Lying nearby is the carrier for an army issue lightweight gasmask. Although the masks were almost always discarded, the carrier was useful as a means of carrying additional personal items. (USMC)

Centre right: A group of Marines unleash a volley of fire from their M1 carbines and Garands on a suspected Japanese position during mopping up operations on Tinian 1944. Draped over the shoulder of the Marine in the center is an SCR-536 'handie-talkie' personal radio, which could be used for communications over short distances. (USMC)

Below: A group of Navy and Marine officers salute the flag as it is raised over Tinian Island in August 1944. The Marine MP at the right has attached his K-Bar fighting knife to his pistol belt. The K-Bar, first issued in 1943, became legendary among Marines. Next to his fighting knife, he has attached a canteen in an army carrier to his belt. The army carrier can be distinguished by the vertical row of stitching and the letters US stencilled to the front. Marine Corps issue gear was not stencilled U.S. (NA)

Left: Marines delicately remove a comrade wounded on Peleliu. The Marine at left has an army issue M-3 fighting knife in an M-8 scabbard attached to his belt. Visible in the foreground of the picture is an M7 grenade launcher, which has been attached to a Garand. The M7 could fire Mk II A1 fragmentation grenades out to ranges of 250 yards. (USMC)

Below: A machine gun crew uses the cover provided by a pile of coral rock to fire on Japanese positions on Peleliu. The gunners are firing the Browning M1919A4 air-cooled .30 caliber machine gun. The thirty-one pound .30 caliber machine gun had a rate of fire of between 450-500 rounds per minute. To maintain that rate of fire, two belts of ammunition, each containing 250 rounds, were carried in metal cans (visible to the left of the gun). (USMC)

Above left: A stretcher party catches its breath near a destroyed Japanese searchlight on Peleliu, September 1944. The Marine at right is wearing a pair of Army leggings. Marine leggings had fewer hooks and eyelets. (USMC)

Above right: Marines prepare to move up on Peleliu. Spare magazines for the Thompson sub machine gun of the Marine at left is carried in the pouch visible on his left side. Next to his canteen, this man has also attached a jungle first aid kit, which appeared towards the end of the war. Unlike the earlier first aid kit, which only contained a bandage and disinfectant, the jungle kit contained a variety of ointments and medicines. (USMC)

Below: Marines of the 4th Division land on Iwo Jima and immediately come under fire. The pattern of the camouflage helmet cover is clearly visible on the Marines in the foreground. The Marine at right has placed his M1 carbine in a plastic bag designed to keep weapons dry during landings. (USN)

Above: A Marine 37mm gun fires on Mount Suribachi. The crew of this gun has cut the armored shield on the front of their gun to break up the shield's silhouette. Extra rounds for the gun are carried in cardboard tubes, visible in the hole behind the gun. The two Marines on the right are wearing the Army field jacket. (USMC)

Below: A T45 rocket launcher mounted on a one-ton truck unleashes a salvo of M8 rockets toward enemy positions on Iwo Jima. Each truck carried three, twelve rocket, launchers. Although able to deliver a great deal of firepower in a short period of time, the rocket launchers, which generated a great deal of smoke, also attracted enemy artillery fire. (USMC)

Above: A well-entrenched Marine 105mm howitzer shells Mount Suribachi. The volcano's commanding view of the island is clearly visible in this picture. The crew of this gun are all wearing the army field jacket. The stencil on the Gerry can just outside of the gun pit is stencilled with the 5th Marine Division's rectangular insignia. This would indicate that this gun was assigned to the Thirteenth Marines, the Fifth 'MarDiv''s artillery regiment. (USMC)

Right: Marines at a position before Mount Suribachi on Iwo Jima, February 1945. The Marine facing the camera at right has the headset for his SCR-300/ BC 1000 man-pack radio, the top of which is visible in front of him. The handset for the radio is visible in his left hand. (NA)

Left: Marine photographer Joseph Rosenthal's picture of Marines raising the flag over Mount Suribachi is arguably the most famous image of World War II. This flag raising was actually the second flag raising on Mount Suribachi. The first involved a flag that was too small to be seen at a great distance. Although this photograph depicts the second flag raising, the photographer did not, as some have asserted, stage it. Of the six men who participated in the flag raising pictured here, only three would survive the battle. (USMC)

Below: Marines pinned down by fire from Suribachi. While the Marines at the top of the slope lay prone just below the horizon, others attempt to dig foxholes. This photograph illustrates the black volcanic sand that was to cause the Marines on Iwo Jima such difficulty. The large square box visible on the back of the Marine immediately behind the foxhole is a special rubberized container used to transport the man-pack radio during landing operations. (USN)

Left: General Holland Smith, standing second from left and Secretary of the Navy James V. Forrestal. Observing the flag raising from a ship of shore, Forrestal turned to Smith and said, '*Holland, the raising of that flag on Suribachi means a Marine Corps for the next five hundred years*'. (USN)

Top right: Combat weary Marines on Iwo Jima display their trophies. They are wearing a variety of clothing. The Marine at left is wearing the M1941 utility cap with a brim pinned up by a bronze Marine Corps insignia. He wearing an army issue HBT fatigue jacket. The Marine at center is wearing the utility cap and a cardigan sweater, while the Marine at right is wearing an army issue knit shirt. The knit shirt was lighter weight than the five-button wool sweater. (USN)

Above: One of eight Marine 'Zippo' tanks deployed on Iwo Jima. The Zippos were M4A3 Sherman tanks that had been equipped with the navy's Mark I flamethrower. The more heavily armored Zippos proved to be more effective than earlier experiments with flamethrower equipped M3 tanks. Wooden planks have been affixed to the side of this vehicle to prevent Japanese soldiers from affixing magnetic mines to the tank. (USMC)

Top left: Among the many jobs that women Marines performed was as airplane mechanics. Here, a group of WMs work on a B-25 Mitchell bomber. The women are all wearing the women's utility coat and forest green garrison caps. The women's utility uniform was similar to the men's, except that it was made of lighter weight cotton and was closed by four composite buttons. (USMC)

Right: A female Marine on leave poses for a picture. She is wearing the forest green service uniform with cordovan leather gloves and handbag. In accordance with regulation, she has covered her lips with 'Montezuma Red' lipstick, a shade developed specifically for women Marines. (KL)

Left: Women Marines salute a Marine Corps color guard. These women are wearing the green and white summer service uniform with the peppermint green summer dress cap. Regulations dictating that women Marine's hair would not fall below the shoulder were strictly enforced.(USMC)

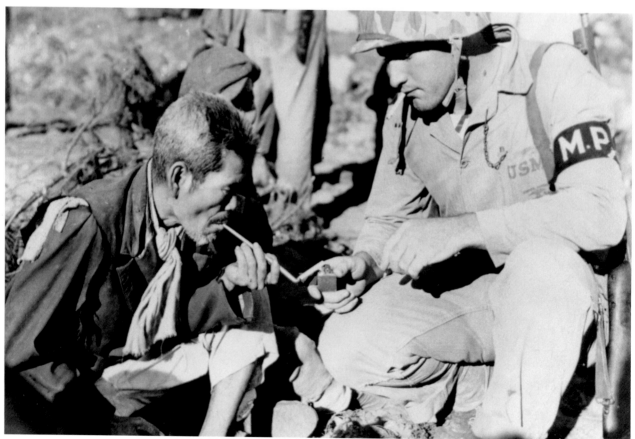

Top left: Two Marines on Okinawa try and reunite a family. The Marine at right is wearing a P1944 herringbone utility cap underneath his M1 helmet. The P1944 cap resembled the earlier 1941 cap, but had a longer bill. On his pack is attached an M1943 folding shovel in its carrier. The M1943 shovel began to reach Marine units in 1944. (USMC)

Bottom left: A Marine M.P. lights a pipe for an elderly Okinawan civilian. He is using a Zippo lighter with the popular black crackle finish. The sturdy Zippo was a privately purchased item that was a favorite of American service personnel during the war. As an M.P. this man has a whistle in his left breast pocket. The whistle is secured to his jacket by a brass chain, which is hooked to the top buttonhole of his jacket. (USMC)

Above: Marines of the 6th Marine Division debark from a LCVP (Landing Craft Vehicle and Personnel), the famous 'Higgins Boat,' at the start of the Okinawa campaign, the last campaign of the war. All of these Marines are wearing sage green utility uniforms with camouflage helmet covers and shelter halves. They present a much more uniformed appearance than would have been found during operations earlier in the war. (USMC)

Below: Movie star Tyrone Power, left, was a Marine pilot during the war. In this photograph Power can be seen wearing the leather G-1 flight jacket, which was worn by both Navy and Marine Corps pilots. He is also wearing a civilian baseball cap. He is speaking with Leif Erickson, who is wearing a Navy deck jacket and herringbone fatigue hat. (USN)

Above: Although the Japanese had already surrendered, the Marines who arrived for occupation duty in September 1945 were prepared for a hostile landing. Here, the second wave of Marines to arrive on Japanese soil disembarks from Higgins boats. The Higgins boat was the mainstay of allied landing parties during the war in every theatre. (NA)

Left: Marines of a ship's detachment stand inspection before landing at Tokyo Bay. All of the men are wearing three pocket HBT utility uniforms. The riflemen have their jackets tucked into their trousers. Interestingly, the platoon sergeant at the front has sewn his insignia to the sleeve of his utility jacket. Rank insignia was generally not sewn to the sleeve of the utility uniform although it was sometimes stencilled to the utility jacket. (USMC)

Above: Three Marines assigned to occupation duty use a phrase book to communicate with Japanese policemen. The two Marines at left have tucked their jackets into their trousers. The Marine at the left has a .45 caliber pistol in a privately acquired holster attached to his M1936 pistol belts. (USMC)

Below: A Marine band strikes up a tune at Sasebo, Japan in September 1945. The men are all wearing utility uniforms with the liner of the M1 helmet. The photograph illustrates the fullness of the fatigue trousers, and the often inaccurate measurements of Marine quartermasters. (USMC)

Above: A Marine on a security patrol in Kyushu passes by a geisha house. A K-bar knife and lensatic compass have been attached to the left side of his pistol belt. (USMC)

Left: A group of Marines on occupation duty in China pose for a photograph. After the Japanese surrender, some Marines were dispatched to China to oversee the demobilization of Japanese troops there. All of these Marines are wearing wool winter service trousers. The man at the center is wearing the wool winter service shirt, which was identical in construction to the cotton service shirt, worn by the Marine at left, only made from wool flannel. The three men in the rear are wearing army issue M1943 field jackets, which began to be issued to Marines after the war had ended. (CJA)

INDEX